First published in Great Britain in 1993 by
ANCHOR BOOKS
1-2 Wainman Road, Woodston,
Peterborough, PE2 7BU

All Rights Reserved

Copyright Contributors 1993

Foreword

Turkey and Mistletoe is a collection of poems based upon the frenzied activity surrounding that special day in the calendar that thank heavens only comes once a year!

Whilst children marvel at the sheer magic of Christmas, anxious parents are desperately working behind the scenes to make the miracle come true.

Also there are the relatives to contend with, all expecting a lavish feast complete with trimmings, prepared by an exhausted mum in a hot steamy kitchen. And from every household you can hear the distant cries of 'No, not turkey again!' as the leftovers are disguised and concocted into different meals to suffice well into the New Year.

All the poems in this book capture the different emotions of the day, the ups and downs and ultimately the sheer magic of Christmas.

Michelle Abbott
Editor

Contents

The Miracle	Pauline Duke	1
Blessings	Enid Rathbone	2
Christmas Child	J N Cates	3
The Christmas Star	Joan Pierce	4
Christmas Eve	Margaret Reardon	5
The First Christmas	Ken Buckley	6
Christmas Cheer	A Saunders	7
A Christmas Legend	Alison Cox	8
Christmas Innocence	Lisa Foggo	9
Christmas	Kevin Dunphy	10
My Christmas Fairy	Muriel Cooper	11
The Light of the World	Jean Maynard	12
Out of Focus	D E Frost	13
A Child's Christmas	Rauline Ransley	14
The Stable	D Townshend	15
Sonnet to the Saviour	Margaret Reynolds	16
The Rubbish Collector	Eamonn Costello	17
Untitled	D E Jones	18
Mandy's Christmas Gift of Love	Avril Houlton	19
Old Harry	Harry Hunter	20
Letter to Santa	Bessie Eden	21
Christmas Joy	M Thorne	22
The Four Kings	Hermione Roff	23
A Christmas Party	Ellen M Walker	24
English Christmas	Norman Hadland	25
Said our Boss Dog to the Cat	Shirley Ann Berrows	26
Christmas Gone?	May Clark	27
The Christmas that Nearly Wasn't	M Young	28
Dear Mum	Alan Catto	29
Pets' Christmas	Maureen Brudenell Masters	30
Untitled	K McCombie	31
Setting the Scene	Tanya Gray	32
To Mum at Christmas	I Allpress	33
All the World Loves Xmas Day	Dorothy Altman	34
The Night Before Christmas	Carole Wright	35

Title	Author	Page
The Christmas Party	Gillian M Thomson	36
Christmas	Frank Vincent	37
The Meaning of Christmas	Valerie Foggo	38
Christmas	M Baxter	39
Children	Bernard Kevin	40
Christmas Time	Hazel Foster	41
A Happy Christmas	Samantha Green	42
Christmas	John L McKeag	43
Christmas	I Smith	44
Oh Why?	Morris Green	45
Christmas Past	Brenda Hudson	46
Santa is Waiting	Cynthia Dickens	47
Untitled	Patricia Feeney	48
The Night Santa Came	Linda Webster	49
For Betsy From Mum and Dad	Barbara Morgan	50
Peeping Tom	Pauline Peachey	51
Children at Christmas	Eleanor Friston	52
The Christmas Snowman	Paul Sanders	53
Santa's Gift List	M Haslam	54
Oh Santa Claus	M Burridge	55
It's Christmas	Sarojini Bertha Peters	56
Snoop	M P Newman	57
Christmas is Here	Sandra Gwilliam	58
Yuletide	Alice McCarroll	59
Visions of Christmas	K Round	60
Boyhood Christmas	W Amos	61
Christmas Eve	Christine Spooner	62
Christmas Here on Earth	A E Norfolk	64
Christmas Shopping	Jean Wallbank	65
A Christmas Box	Jim Armstrong	67
Xmas Eve	Eve Calder	68
The Time of Year	M Truepenny	69
The Xmas Tree	D Baynes	70
Christmas	Doris Riding	71
Christmas Ghosts	Margery Horsburgh	72
Humour	Mary Whittle	73

Title	Author	Page
Oh! Lord is Christmas Here Again Already?	Caren Jayne	74
Why Fairies Top our Christmas Tree	Colin Willis	75
Untitled	Mary Bell	76
Christmas Crackers	E Haydon Sanderson	77
The Dog's DInner	Margaret Smythers	78
Christmas Day	Stephen Norris	79
Wrong Day	R L Bennett	80
Tarnished Tinsel	Sue Caple	81
The Present	John Wellings	82
A Teenage Hero Father Christmas	Robert Hougton	83
Oozing with Christmas Spirit?!	Tony Watson	84
Christmas Humour	Erimar MacMillan	85
Xmas Shopping	Caroline Shore	86
Christmas Shopping	Mona Bulmer	87
A Very Happy Christmas	J Roberts	88
The Real Story	Alison Downie	89
Christmas Day Visit	G Price	90
The Christmas Tree	Rita Vincent	91
News Flash	Sue Bevin	92
Untitled	Anne Lamb	93
Untitled	Christine Rodgers	94
Warmest Wishes	Michael L G Bailey	95
Things That Go Jump in the Night	E Spinks	96
A Thought for Xmas	Clare Barnett	97
Three Wishes	Norma Tate	98
Christmas Lunch at the Day Hospital	Gwen Barton	99
An Orphans Wish	Janis Robertson	100
To Kevin at Christmas	Raine Marriner	101
Suffer Little Children	Roy Whitfield	102
Once Again	J Nice	103
Dear Father Christmas	Jan Lowe	104
What Can I Get?	Margaret Aitken	105
Christmas Humour	Muriel Palmer	106

The Fairy	June Linacre	107
Untitled	Julie March	108
Delilah II	K Chesney-Woods	109
Christmas Day 1962	P Durow	110
Star Glazing at Christmas	David Bratley	111
Untitled	P Gordon	112
Father Christmas	L K Webster	113
Christmas Tribute to Dad	Kevin E Sims	114
Advent Hopes	J Wright	115
Mother Alone	Barbara Eassom	116
Untitled	E Dall	117
A Young Boy's Secret	David Quick	118
Christmas Eve	Ruby Anderson	119
Seasons	Grace Clark	120

The Miracle

A baby cried - a sleepy Mother stirred;
Awake now, she marvelled at what she heard,
She held tiny fingers - touched soft, downy head,
And covered him close, in a manger, his only bed.
Gentle-eyed oxen, quiet donkey, and sheep
Nuzzle and nudge the babe - now again fast asleep.
Outside, the night so cold, the wind so shrill,
But inside, contentment; warm and still.
A bright lone star shines high in the skies
And leads to the place where the new babe lies;
Great men and shepherds - rich men and poor,
All bring their offerings - all kneel in awe,
They gaze with humility - in silent adoration,
For here is the new King - promised to the Nation.
Long ago came that Baby - our Saviour - to Earth,
But still today we wonder - at the miracle of Birth.

Pauline Duke

Blessings

On Christmas Night, I wish you - Love,
And hope that you'll express,
This wonderful ingredient
That makes true happiness.

On Christmas Night, I wish you - Joy
With fun, and light, and laughter.
And music, merriment, good friends,
Remembering hereafter.

On Christmas Night, I wish you - Peace.
A blessing set apart.
That happiness and sweet content
Will ever fill your heart.

On Christmas Night, I wish you - Safe,
And on your homeward way,
I hope that you'll remember
A very happy day.

And at this Holy Christmastide
I ask you to recall
That God's own son was born on Earth
The reason for it all.

Enid Rathbone

Christmas Child

Sleep Christmas child sleep
Slumber in the wonder
Of your first awaking light,
New life always precious is
A multitude of miracles
When born at Christmas tide.

Hush Christmas child hush
You may hear the crooning yet of angels,
Singing sweet hosannas
To the wonder of new life.

Stay Christmas child stay
Remain a babe my sweet one,
Tomorrow is a world of growing up,
Hold on to your innocence
Small miracle of love.

Dream Christmas child dream
Your room is not a stable bare
Your cot a manger not,
You may grow into a king,
Or yet, the Prince of Love.

J N Cates

The Christmas Star

If you look out of your window,
On a dark winter's night,
You could just see the Christmas Star
All shiny silver and bright.
It was this same twinkling star,
That lit the wise men on their way,
For they had heard a babe was born far far away.
Bringing gifts of gold frankincense and myrrh
Soon they saw the stable and knew that they were near.
For laying in a manger, now all snug and warm
It was the place in Bethlehem where Jesus Christ was born.
We may not be so lucky to have gifts so rare,
But around us at Christmas we have those who really care
For that twinkling star in heaven is still shiny bright
looking down upon us making everything just right.

Joan Pierce

Christmas Eve

The wintry winds did howl and blow,
And in its wake brought feathery snow.
Each small window threw rays of light,
Making pathways silvery bright,
Inside warm fires burned red and glowed,
White shadows played round mistletoe.
Children danced and laughed with glee,
To see the dazzling Christmas tree.
Outside the people wrapped up warm,
Singing in chorus Christ is born.
Church bells echoed loud and clear,
Telling the world the Lord is here
Oh happy, happy Christmastide
Goodwill and peace to all mankind.

Margaret Reardon

The First Christmas

Choir boys singing in the glistening snow.
Their faces shining in the lanterns' glow.
And borne upon the wintry wind, the sound
of church bells ringing.

They sing of shepherd who watched by night.
And of the star that shone so bright.
Guiding the wise men who had travelled far.
Their gifts to the stable bringing.

They sing of a babe in a manger sleeping.
With guardian angels their vigil keeping.
They tell of how it began in a humble stall
They sing of the very first Christmas of all.

Ken Buckley

Christmas Cheer

People will be singing
Carols in the morn
Rejoicing the birth of Jesus
Who many years ago was born

It was a time of happiness
And wise men came along
Bringing presents for the baby
For Virgin Mary had a son.

Now we all have presents
Brought by Santa Claus
On that great day in December,
The twenty fifth day of course.

So I wish you a happy Christmas
And remember the teaching of Jesus the Son
Showing kindness and love
To each and everyone.

A Saunders

A Christmas Legend

High in the still and starry sky
A silhouette appears,
'Tis Santa with his magic sleigh
And craggy-horned reindeers.
Whilst we are sleeping, dreaming dreams
Of happiness and pleasure
The spiders creep, and contemplate
The tree with all its treasure.
Sweet-scented pine so laden down
With baubles, bells, and toys.
The spiders plan an extra treat
For sleeping girls and boys.
On lanky legs they twist and spin
A web of finest lace
Then, gently, Jesus touches them
And in the grey webs place
Hang silver strands and golden strands
And strands of every hue.
May the miracle of Christmas joy
Shine its holy light on you.

Alison Cox

Christmas Innocence

The presents sit underneath the tree,
The Church speaks out, saying 'Peace to thee.'
The holly is brightening up the wall,
A child was born, coming for us all.

The cards we send, to our many friends,
Santa comes down, there can be no frowns,
The lights are bright, robins are in flight,
Carols we sing, while the church bells ring.

Lisa Foggo

Christmas

Now is the time, to make amends
Now is the time, to seek a friend
Where you can share, your joy, and laughter
And hopefully, keep forever after

This is the season, for all concerned
Where good examples, should be learned
When each in turn, will show the way
That a little kindness, is here to stay

Remembering the saviour child, born to save us all
To give us grace and strength, ere we fall
We should but always, try our best
And then in time, we will pass the test

So let us all rise, to energise our natures, as they unfold
Bringing forth new ideas, thus amply told
Only then we will understand, and learn to reason
The beauty and happiness of this eternal season.

Kevin Dunphy

My Christmas Fairy

The fairy on my Christmas tree
Is tattered and she's worn,
My Mother brought her long ago
The year that I was born,
She's seen a lot of ups and downs
And many tears as well,
I wish that she could only talk
All the tales she'd have to tell,
My Daddy died so long ago,
When I was still quite young,
But every year at Christmas time
On the tree the fairy hung,
Once her small wand shone very bright
But now I'm sad to say,
As I look at her upon my tree
She almost seems to have had her day,
But never mind perhaps next year
I'll make her a brand new dress,
For to part with her, would break my heart,
I really must confess.

Muriel Cooper

The Light of the World

The light of the World brings forth such joy,
And throughout the ages it's been known,
By the seeds of our Lord which is continually sown,
Created as such by the birth of this boy.
Who changed our hearts in many ways,
Towards a clearer understanding of one's own mind,
Of how Love has been shown and what it conveys,
When the spirit within is spread by his kind.
Lord of Lord, King of Kings, Jesus brought forth a fine new
                                                                  beginning.
Nestled upon this humble ground, he clutched his mother's hand,
And gently gurgled whilst the Earth was singing,
As Christmas took hold of our land.
So blessed are those who's feelings are there,
To be continued along life's way,
For it's a wonderful joy that we all can share,
On this glorious Christmas Day.

Jean Maynard

Out of Focus

Christmas comes but once a year,
And with it comes good cheer,
For some just like to eat and drink,
While others kneel in prayer.

For me it is a solemn time,
The birth of Christ the King.
A time to pray, and time to think of the babe in Bethlehem.

We all indulge we have our fun, to celebrate Yuletide,
But do we ever stop to think, of three wise men, the star, or child.

So celebrate this Christmas time go ahead and have your fun
But spare a thought for the Son of God who was born in Bethlehem.

D E Frost

A Child's Christmas

Can you enter the Land of Make Believe,
Read the mind of a child, on Christmas Eve,
Recall waking early on Christmas morn,
Before the approach of the wintry dawn.

Now my children hasten to say goodnight,
They are looking so starry eyed, and bright,
With ecstatic faces raised for a kiss,
I can well imagine their halcyon bliss.

For in reverie and meditation,
I still feel that magical elation.

It's lovely to wander down Memory Lane,
To become in one's heart a child again.
So, as I journey along life's way,
A fervent prayer to the Lord, I say.

I pray for all children everywhere,
That their Yuletide shall be as happy and fair,
As the ones I spent in the long ago.
With presents and parties, holly and snow,
But may they remember all else above,
The Christmas Spirit of kindness and love.

Pauline Ransley

The Stable

Safe in the stable where animals low
Away from the wind and freezing cold snow . . .
Their shelter is poor and light is dim,
But Mary and Joseph watch over Him.

Animals gaze at this wondrous sight
Sharing their stable this holy night!
He has no bed . . . just a rough manger
For this little child, this Blessed Stranger.

This precious baby born in a stable
Lying on hay in His manger cradle
Is our dear Lord, who will save us from sin,
So unlock your hearts and let Jesus in!

D Townshend

Sonnet to the Saviour

Welcome to the Father's Son
He whose life has just begun,
Already he our heart has won
By the way he looks and the things he's done,
Wishing him a lot of fun,
Success and happiness by the ton,
For him the penny and the bun,
His Father's gifts, the ad lib pun
Sweet child the Heavenly Father's Son
Hoping that the stars and sun
Shine on Him 'til days are done,
Understanding where and where upon,
Sinless and most perfect one
Mary's *God incarnate Son.*

Margaret Reynolds

The Rubbish Collector

There once was an old man we use too know
He lived nearby just down the road
Everyday he collected old toys and rags
Some say his house was filled with big red bags
Now this old man he had some boys
All through the night making lots of noise
In the day when he went out
The house was silent not a single shout.

This old man was very very old
Along white beard and a heart of gold
When December comes and the first falls of snow
The old man would disappear and go
He loves the children so very much
This old man never loses touch
We do not know where he goes
But I bet you kids can hear his sleigh bells.

Eamonn Costello

Untitled

Christmas trees are shining bright
Kiddies singing Silent Night
Snow is falling on the ground
People busy running round
Robin red breast snow and holly
It's the time for feeling jolly
A mince pie and milk is made ready
For Santa with his sack so heavy
Kiddies excited they cannot sleep
In his sack they'd love to peep
Reindeers rushing as they go
Through the streets in wind and snow
Once in Royal David City
Houses trees decorated pretty
Lots of gifts loads of toys
For all the little girls and boys
Turkey stuffing Christmas pud
All of this if you are good
Christmas Day will soon be here
Merry Christmas and a happy
New Year.

D E Jones

Mandy's Christmas Gift of Love

Mandy was twenty and believed in Santa Claus.
She was mentally handicapped of course.
Making cards and baubles, the excitement showing,
Singing carols, her brown eyes glowing.
She loved to watch a nativity play,
About Jesus, born on Christmas Day.
Gathering holly, decorating the tree,
Baking mince-pies for Christmas tea.
Simple gifts filled her with joy,
A jigsaw, a book, a cuddly toy.
She's gone now, but the gift she left behind,
Was the love she felt for all mankind.

Avril Houlton

Old Harry

Christmas nineteen twenty one
Was a great occasion for everyone.
That's the time when I was born,
A little boy child snug and warm.
Not quite as famous as the other boy though
Born in a stable two thousand years ago.
But all the same, with love and care
We both lived long enough to share
Some happiness with friends we knew
Until the hate and violence grew
I don't think I'll be such a loss
As the one that died upon the cross.

Harry Hunter

Letter to Santa

Dear Santa Claus, I wish to know,
If you can get here, in the snow,
My room is at the top of the stairs,
I am a good boy, and say my prayers,
If you can't make it, on your sleigh,
It won't be the same on Xmas Day,
If other children need you more,
I'll understand, I won't be sore,
I am lucky, and I know it.
Make them happy, they will show it.
I can see the snowflakes drifting down
Covering our dear old town.
Love's abounding in our house
Quiet and silent like a mouse,
Please Santa, try your best,
You'll put my patience to the test,
Happy Christmas everyone,
If you can't come, we'll still have fun.

Bessie Eden

Christmas Joy

I dreamt that it was Christmas
and around the Christmas tree
exciting gifts all gaily wrapped
each one a mystery.

Dressed warmly in my fur lined coat
feeling all aglow
I marvelled at the wonderland
created by winter's snow.

On entering the deserted park
through the sparse branches I did see
a beggar boy in threadbare clothes,
shivering, he smiled at me.

This pathetic, frozen figure
did beckon me his way,
looking beautiful and radiant
as in the snow he knelt to pray.

'Peace, and every Christmas joy
I extend to everyone.'
With outstretched hands he vanished,
as His words did linger on.

My dream abruptly ended,
but forever there will be
the two of us at Christmas
my beggar boy, and me.

M Thorne

The Four Kings

Gold splashes its light boldly, to and fro,
Flickering and reflecting its age-old wisdom, as
One King recognises another. He draws close the
More to shine within Your encircling orb. He
Thrills at the splendour no gold on Earth can surpass.
Thrills, as The Word from ages past, creates in him anew.
(Another light, another time.)

Frankincense, the word lingers like the curling
Smoke of candles guttering in the wind. His
Prayers, like sighs, shudder and faint at the
Intimate knowledge of such Kingship, such
Power, such glory, set before him, face to face.
(Another face, another time.)

But it is the third King I think of.
Did he break the precious casket of
Myrrh, over Your tiny feet
So that the house was full of the
Fragrance? In his wisdom did he anoint You
Tenderly, and weeping, cover Your infant body with his
Tears, wipe Your soft limbs with his hair?
Every time Mary drew in that scent it
Pierced her with the keenness of its fragrant homage.
(Another Mary, another time.)

And I too, yearn, my Lord, my King, my God, to
Savour You, taste You, as did those Kings.
(Another year, another time.)
To reflect the gold of Your presence in this
Darkened world. Pray, the love prayer of
Frankincense, share the grievous joy of myrrh
Deep in the knowledge of Your wisdom.
This year, this time.

Hermione Roff

A Christmas Party

The Christmas tree was wearing green,
the loveliest dress you've ever seen.
Bows of silver, a touch of red,
a bright shining star on top of her head.
Frosty the Snowman, in dazzling white,
was truly a most impressive sight.
When, rocking and rolling with the -
Tripped over her wand, he had drunk too much sherry!

Rudolph the reindeer, switched on his red nose,
just making sure it really could glow.
The rest of the reindeer, bells gaily ringing,
soon had the other guests happily singing.

Then along came Santa, dressed all in red,
with white fur trimmings and a nicely curled beard.
He led them in a Conga - all around the room.
You should have seen them dancing to the really swinging tunes.

With balloons and crackers, coloured streamers too,
it really was some party, quite a hullabaloo.
They all had such a wonderful time, on this they all agreed.
The night they were rehearsing - *the magic of Christmas Eve!*

Ellen M Walker

English Christmas

I'd heard you tell
Of carols sweetly sung
By the faithful come
To Church in Dingley Dell

I had to come and see
Your English Christmas
Joy; peace, the
Baubled, lighted tree

Great expectations of
Plum pudding all ablaze
Following the feast
Of fleshy festive geese

And lo! Cousin Joe
Uncle Jack and Nellie
Greetings! Welcome!
What's on Telly?

Norman Hadland

Said our Boss Dog to our Cat

'You know that it's Christmas. So come on with me.
Into the lounge, and I'll show you the tree.
Someone's put presents all nice and neat.
And with a good bit of sniffing. We might smell something sweet.

What do you reckon then! Is the smallest one yours?
And how will you open it, with your very soft paws?
Shall I just bark? and let them know that we know.
Or shall we pretend? and pass-by on tiptoe.
Let's curl up here, and get off to sleep.
And at the first sight of dawn, I'll get to work with my teeth.
Isn't it exciting for you and for me?
And we don't have to help to dress up the tree.

When I'm reincarnated, I'm coming back as a dog!
I don't think I'd like to be a hedgehog.
Well, that's me sorted out. But how about you!
'Yes, I think I'll be a dog too.'

Shirley Ann Berrows

Christmas Gone?

Now that Christmas has been and gone,
and the new year on the way,
what will the year hold for us no one
can honestly say,
We make resolutions and promises
galore but very often they fade and die
like many gone before,
I have regrets as I've gone through life
of things not done and said,
so now I've made my mind up to get
to grips with life, and do the best I can
to face each day with courage or
whatever life demands.

May Clark

The Christmas that Nearly wasn't

Christmas cooking smells wafted from the kitchen.
Mysterious presents surrounded the tree.
Santa would come tonight, now James remembered,
As he shuffled and sighed in bored misery.

What if he were early? the eight year old thought;
His heart missed a beat as he pondered with glee.
Upstairs he scampered, but no sack beheld him,
The answer was simple: keep checking to see.

Bedtime came late: Santa may have forgotten.
Surely he came not the same time every year?
Slumber would never come; James knew it could not.
Yet when the dawn called, the lad woke bathed in blear!

Mum and Dad hurried when they heard the tumble,
Finding their son sprawled, his face glowing smiles.
Looking around, gifts and goodies abounded:
How could he forget The Day (birth of God's child)?

Laughter abounds at the family memory,
Recalling the Christmas Day so nearly missed.
Young people learn from James' mishap encountered;
Patience will easier bring all you could wish.

M Young

Dear Mum

Dear Mum, I have a problem,
My problem is Santa Claus,
You know the man with the white beard,
Who by the time you get up has already disappeared,
The man with the black boots
Who never leaves a speck of soot.

Dear Mum, I have a problem,
My problem is Granny and Granda,
You know that their present is always the same,
For the most boring present is their fame,
Last year it was a yellow jumper,
On the front is a picture of Granda's dumper.

Dear Mum, I have a problem,
My problem is Christmas,
I never get the present I want,
Last year I wanted the video *Man Hunt*,
Instead I got *The Little Runt*,
I liked it when Mike came,
So in fact I like Christmas all the same.

Alan Catto

Pets' Christmas

There's a funny little mouse,
In a funny little house,
With a funny little grin,
On his funny little chin.

He tips his funny hat,
To a funny little cat,
And they both shout 'Hip Hooray',
And have a fun-filled Christmas Day.

Maureen Brudenell Masters

Untitled

Oh Santa is jolly, he is big and he is round,
As Christmas approaches you will see him around,
Ringing his bell and shouting ho! ho! ho! with glee
Being very happy for all to see.

On Christmas Eve with his reindeers, he will set out
Flying in the sky all through the night,
Delivering presents for each girl and boy
So that their Christmas will be full of joy.

As daylight approaches, back home he will be,
Having a well earned rest, and a cup of tea.

K McCombie

Setting the Scene

The children are sound asleep in bed
With dreams of Santa in their heads.
There is sherry and mince pies near the door
And presents scattered on the floor.
The tree with lanterns lights the hall,
Christmas cards decorate the once bare walls.
The kitchen is full of Yuletide cheer.
Turkey, nuts, Christmas pudding and beer.
Their stockings are filled with coins and fruit
And Grandad's wearing a Santa suit.
Christmas comes but once a year,
Starts off happy - ends in tears.

Tanya Gray

To Mum at Christmas

To Mum at Christmas we say 'Thank you'.
It seems inadequate, but Mothers do not look for thanks.
Each task is done with love.
In our house Christmas starts in October
when damsons and sloes ripen, ready to make the Christmas cheer.
Puddings are mixed - who wants a stir? make a wish -
Stir stir stir in all that happened through the year.
The cake is made, marzipaned and iced,
Presents are bought and hidden away to surprise.
Where are the decorations, time we got some new ones.
At last all is ready, it's Christmas Eve!
The house is scrubbed, polished and garnished -
Holly, ivy and mistletoe -
The crib set by the window near the lamp.
Could the sky please squeeze out a snowflake or two
Just to make it perfect.
Midnight Mass is over, Mum sits down to take off her new shoes
And tries a sip of her new Christmas brew.
To Mum at Christmas we say 'thank you,' and every other time.

I Allpress

All the World Loves Xmas Day

All the world loves Xmas Day
People near and far away
Every door is open wide
To welcome a new Xmas tide
Everyone like you and me
Love the magic of the tree
With each gift we gladly part
There's Christmas in everyone's heart
With so many memories of each passing year
To hold from the Xmas before
Those memories so lovely so warm and sincere
Will last from the Xmas before
All the world loves Xmas Day
Gladness sorrow come what may
We'll rejoice without a care
For Xmas will always be there!

Dorothy Altman

The Night Before Christmas

Mistletoe white hanging up on the night,
before Christmas,
the children I can still hear their whispers.

Red glowing fire, crackling in the hearth,
was that Father Christmas, who let out a laugh?
little messages left for him,
tot of brandy, and a mince pie.
Not forgetting the reindeers,
who fly in the sky.

The night is so clear with starry jet sky,
white snow flakes that slowly flutter by,
I'm sure I saw the outline of his sleigh?

Snuggled down now at the end of the day,
mother sings carols to us, and she gives us a choice,
she is good with her clear cool voice.
Our eyes are full and bright,
and we are tucked in for the night,
to open our presents the next day,
Oh! what sheer delight.

Carole Wright

The Christmas Party

There were streamers hanging from the walls,
Balloons and bows were strung.
A tree stood proudly in the corner
And on its boughs the presents hung.

A table nestled in the corner,
Spread with lovely food.
There were trifles, chocolate cakes and buns.
It really looked so good.

The children rushed into the room,
Excitement on their faces.
They started off with guessing games
And then they had some races.

The party soon came to an end,
Each had a piece of cake.
They chose a present from the tree
And a party bag they were to take.

They bade farewell to everyone
And homeward bound were led.
The happy tired children
Were soon tucked up in bed.

Gillian M Thomson

Christmas

Presents, cards, tags and wrappings,
Cakes, sweets, food with all the trappings.
Visits, visitors, parties, drinks, yet more food,
Videos, films, photographs all to be viewed.
Perhaps this year while we have a ball
We'll remember it's the time of goodwill to all,
Of others with nothing and no-one to share
And perhaps we'll find time to show that we care.
Then in amongst the joy and the mirth
We might even remember the Holy Birth,
After all that's what it is all about, isn't it?

Frank Vincent

The Meaning of Christmas

Children, now it's Christmas, you're excited,
With glittering tinsel you're delighted.
You wait with joyful expectation,
For Santa's gifts; what jubilation!
But will you recall the shepherds who knelt
In the stable where God also dwelt?
Where angels brought their news of joy
About the birth of a tiny boy.
Will you remember the journey made,
Trailing a star which would never fade
'Til safely it reached the scene of the birth,
The lowest place to be found on Earth?
Where even the Kings knelt to the child,
Heavenly son of a mother mild,
And offered in true humbleness,
Their gifts to Him, in thankfulness.
Will you recall why we celebrate
The birth of a child, so kind and great,
Amidst the grabbing materialism,
The fairy lights and their coloured prisms?

Valerie Foggo

Christmas

We all love Christmas don't we?
This season of goodwill.
When we hear, the Church bells,
And ringing of the tills - that sound
in the basement of all department stores.
That all have a *grotto* for dear old Santa Claus!
They want computer games, and coloured televisions too.
He will promise anything, to make their dreams come true.
A little unsophisticated tot, just wants a bridal doll.
Not one that walks and talks, and needs a nappy change
She's seen one on TV, it's the latest craze.
Let's hope they get what they want.
Mam and Dad not too tuned out!
That's, after all what Christmas is all about!

M Baxter

Children

Santa has not been yet
On this fine Christmas Day
The glow of the lights on the
Christmas tree
The holly and the mistletoe
The smell of fruit from the bowl
Sweets and chocolate on the table
There is a parcel lying in the hall
At last Santa has arrived
Placing parcels around the tree
Filling stockings one two three
The sound of happy voices and music
Will be heard soon
Coming from the children
But Santa has gone to the house next door
Merry Christmas everyone

Bernard Kevin

Christmas Time

Christmas time - it brings us joy
When church bells start to ring,
The children wait for Santa Claus
Their presents he will bring.

A teddy bear - a train set?
Beneath the Christmas tree?
All lit up with fairy lights
For everyone to see.

A cosy room - with mum and dad
A feast to celebrate,
When the children go to bed
Dear Santa's never late.

As soon as Christmas Day arrives
You hear sweet carols sung,
Everyone is joyful
It's time to have some fun.

Children open presents
They've wished and waited for,
We thank the Lord - for everything
Whether rich - or poor.

Hazel Foster

A Happy Christmas

Golden bells cheerfully ringing
Beautiful angels softly dancing,
Silvery stars gently twinkling
Golden fairies prettily twirling,
Silvery tinsel softly hanging
Colourful baubles daintily swaying,
Frosty snowflakes gently spinning
Cheerful fairies daintily shining.

Samantha Green (11)

Christmas

Christmas Eve is a time of joy
When snow falls on the Lea,
With frost adorning the holly tree
A pleasure for all to see.

Christmas is for Santa Clause
and when fairy tales unfold,
of Santa's home in Iceland
and his happy reindeer band.

With presents heaped upon his sleigh
With beard and robe of red,
He'll visit all the children
As they lay asleep in bed.

Bringing wonderment and magic
to lots of sleepy heads.
Toddlers wanting cuddly toys
computors for the bigger boys.

Then comes the dawn
He'd slip away
to journey north on his empty sleigh,
Happy to have given so much fun
Once more his Christmas duties done.

John L McKeag

Christmas

Christmas carols are heard once more
As children go from door to door,
They walk through snow with lanterns held high
As the star of Bethlehem shines down from the sky.

Later on they're tucked up in bed
To wait for Santa who comes on his sledge,
They lie awake to try to peep
But Santa won't come till they're asleep.

Morning comes and they run downstairs
To find lots of toys piled up on the chairs,
Christmas comes but once a year
So for Mum's and Dad's we give three cheers.

I Smith

Oh Why?

Children of all ages
Full of delight
Christmas is here
Joy to the ear.

Toys big and small
Bring smiles to them all
Peace is shattered
Wrappings battered.

The son of God
Beholds the scene
Delights in the glow
Of an answered dream.

The world is at peace
Enjoying the feast
Oh why could we not
Have Christmas a lot.

Morris Green

Christmas Past

Anna-Marie stood on tip toe
Gazing longingly into the lighted shop window
'Let me see too,' lisped younger William
'Is there a 'Farver Crismuss?'

Anna-Marie held him up -
'Oohs and ahs came thick and fast
As the children's imagination ran riot
And eager eyes were cast on the
Crepe paper crackers, baubles, tinsel and such.
Mysterious parcels - toy's they yearned to touch

The sweet shop was next - festive wrapped to entice
Fancy boxes be-ribboned, bringing seasonal delight
'I'll have liquorice strings,' sighed Anna-Marie
                              or perhaps chocolate drops
'What's your choice little William
Those pretty pink and white sugar mice?'

There was no money for such frippery
But the children's dreams that night
Were star spangled like the magic of Christmas.

Brenda Hudson

Santa is Waiting

Hush! You children now tucked up in bed,
Why are you not asleep?
Dear Santa's waiting with his sack,
He'll not come if you peep.

The elves can take a well earned rest,
They've toiled so hard and long
Creating gifts for every child,
They've worked with will and song.

The reindeer now pull Santa's sleigh,
They skim the roof tops high;
So close your eyes, dear children do,
Or they will pass you by.

The Christmas bells ring loud and clear,
It's getting very late:
You should be in the land of dreams
For Santa's at your gate.

Now Santa is a busy man,
He's lots of visits to make;
So dream of the gifts he's bringing for you
And the joy when you awake.

Cynthia Dickens

Untitled

It's nearly Christmas hear Lucy say
I cannot wait for Christmas day.
Christmas tree's and coloured lights
Twinkle, twinkle, 'o' so bright.
Lucy looked up to the sky
A thousand stars away up high,
It's just like Christmas up there to
Little angels and maybe Winnie the Pooh.
All kinds of shapes and different size
It's night-time now, we close our eyes.
'Wake up, wake up,' hear Lucy say
the snow is here, it's Christmas day.
Lots of presents, lots of food
Santa knew that I was good,
All them presents under the tree
Are they really all for me?
Lucy was feeling happy and gay
Hooray, hooray, it's Christmas day!

Patricia Feeney

The Night Santa Came

There wasn't a sound in the house.
But Natalie couldn't sleep.
She felt too excited.
Lying quietly in her bed,
She said some prayers instead.
Thinking of the baby, Jesus,
Natalie drifted off to sleep.
A few hours later,
Someone special came to her door.
Opened it gently and took a peep,
Then saw her fast asleep.
So, placed on the floor, by the bed,
A sack, filled with toys.
Later, when she awoke,
Her eyes were bright with delight.
She saw so many presents.
It was a splendid sight.
Santa had been busy last night.
Doing his work in a dim light.

Linda Webster

For Betsy From Mum and Dad

It is Xmas Eve and quite late
We peer in your room an d we see
You stand by the window and watch
Just like us, long ago, and you say
Tonight I *will* stay awake
and see him arrive in his sleigh.
The happy old man with white beard
and coat of bright holly red
The garden is strange, for the snow
Has covered the plants and the lawn
And the trees are jet-black
In the light of a silvery moon.
But it's *cold!*
I'll creep into bed for a warm.

I open my eyes and I see at the end of the bed
Parcels of various shapes
And a stocking entrancingly full.

I've missed him *again!*

Barbara Morgan

Peeping Tom

The longest night ever is Christmas Eve
We are far too excited to sleep
We wait for the hush when all are in bed
To tiptoe downstairs - for a peep!

The clock in the hall strikes a quarter to two
And we open the sitting room door
Standing before us the tree all dressed up
With presents beneath, on the floor.

So lovingly wrapped with ribbons and bows
'To Katy and Tom from Aunt Molly'
A splendid red engine for six year old Tom
For Katy, a sweet cuddly dolly.

We crept back to bed eyes heavy with sleep
We've peeped without anyone knowing
Not only the day we longed for is here
Hooray - while we slept, its been snowing!

Pauline Peachey

Children at Christmas

Tinsel sparkling on the tree
Tell me children what do you see?
Lights abound, above the sound
Of excitement and activity
Looking, longing for Christmas Day
Oh! Mum!, will it ever come?
I can hardly wait to see,
My gifts unwrapped at the Christmas tree.
Now I wonder if Dad forgot
To get me a hoop, or whip and top.
Or a fluffy monkey on a string,
Oh! I want just about everything,
But the greatest gift is already mine,
I don't need to look under the tree,
For with me every day of my life,
Is my wonderful family.

Eleanor Friston

The Christmas Snowman

The snowman began to melt as snowmen always do,
First his hat and cane fell down, then his carrot nose fell too.
His black coal eyes began to sink into the melting snow,
As buttons fell from off his coat onto the ground below.

Soon the snowman vanished into the warmer ground,
And no-one could remember what he looked like when around.
But when next Christmas came along, a strange thing happened
                                                                          then,
I looked up at the hillside and there he was again!

Paul Sanders

Santa's Gift List

Santa Claus is most confused,
As Christmas Eve draws near,
He's looking at the list of gifts,
For children far and near.

It used to be all trains and dolls,
For books and model ships,
But now it's computers, digitals, microchips,
Poor old Santa, it's giving him the pip.

He belongs with Dickens
Not modern, he's despondent,
Will some younger chap take over?
And let him be redundant.

M Haslam

Oh Santa Claus

Oh! Santa Claus
Every year you come down the chimney
Gifts for everyone some for him, her and us
Oh! Santa Claus
Do you ever think of yourself
Don't you ever celebrate Christmas
Do you sometimes wish
That you could leave your reindeer
And stop and catch the bus
Don't you ever wish instead of the snow, wind and rain
That you could go surfing
In the hot Mediterranean plane
Or that the Christmas spirit
Would be bigger than the flame
On a Christmas pud
Or stay in a bottle where it should
Oh! Santa wouldn't it be nice
If your outfit of cherry red
Could be psychedelic instead
If this were the case Santa Claus please stay in bed

M Burridge

It's Christmas

When the snow
   falls snow on snow
And the cold winds
   blow on, blow
It's sure that Christmas
   Is around once more.

There!
   It brings:-
   Long icicles hanging;
   Sleigh bells ringing;
   Choirs carol-singing;
   Church bells chiming;
   People rejoicing,
And for the children
   Presents galore
   On the floor
Under the Christmas Tree

Sarojini Bertha Peters

Snoop

Do you know where your presents are
I've found mine, don't you know
I've got books and games and a dolls pram
And a glass thing that looks like snow.

I've got clothes and shoes and ribbons
Felt pens and colouring books
Now I know everything that I've got
I wish I hadn't looked.

M P Newman

Christmas is Here

Holly, tinsel, mistletoe,
Fairy lights and candle glow,
Rich plum pudding, Christmas cake,
Trying hard to stay awake.
Secrets - whispering on the stair,
Wrapping paper, frosty air;
Balloons and streamers in my room,
Carol singers, out of tune.
'Christmas is here,' they gaily sing.
I wonder - what will Santa bring.

Sandra Gwilliam

Yuletide

Yesterday was Christmas Eve;
Uproar! Chaos reigned supreme!
Lovely! Christmas! Day of feasting
Even for the diet eating.

Toys are scattered all around
In the kitchen plates abound
Dad will do the washing up
Every Mum has *her* feet up.

Alice McCarroll

Visions of Christmas

Children's eyes glisten at baubles of gold.
Gossamer moonbeams smile softly *hello*.
Melodies linger: happy, mellow, cold
Come All Ye Faithful! concerted and low.

People hear music: soft baubles of snow.
Cheeks are more rosy: Christmas so near.
Sable-eyed robin his breast is aglow:
Bells of Christmas resound welcoming cheer.

Beauty of crystals in tinsel - like veil,
Kissed by snow storm: April - like showers
Chameleon shapes lamp-posts of stone hail,
Vying snow schools of imps stepping rose flowers

Some of the visions of Christmas to be,
Home is the place, the family to see.

K Round

Boyhood Christmas

When a boy, I knew the fog and cold
On the way to school at twelve years old.
Across the Forest in bitter sleet
Hurried to school down icy street.

At Christmas time the story told
The Scrooge and Marley tale unfold.
I read the story through and through
Imagination made it true.

Going home in winter dark
The Dickens story made its mark.
Every door I saw the ghastly face
Or long dead Marley cap and lace.

Home at last and a slice of toast
And bread and jam for tea.
Put gaudies on the Christmas Tree
Saw Mum prepare tomorrow's roast.

I sang the Carol on Christmas Eve
Went to Church across the way.
Had Christmas fare on Christmas Day
Played indoor games the family way.

W Amos

Christmas Eve

When all is still and dark around
And there isn't even a sound,
That's when the toys all come to life
Dolly Teddy and his wife.
Clockwork soldiers all in a row
March up and down and to and fro,
Drums and trumpets all come out
Books and puzzles begin to shout.
For last year's toys are having a fling
Before they hear those jingle bells ring,
Santa Claus is on his way
And soon they will be put away.
They won't be needed for a while
They can only watch the children smile,
For they will have new toys Christmas morn
And all be up at the crack of dawn,
To find the new toys Christmas brings
And they will only be *old* things.

Christine Spooner

Christmas Here on Earth

Christmas comes but once a year
Thank God for that some say.
What with presents to buy and cards to send
Funds don't go a long way.

The shops are loud and noisy
Long before Advent has come
And the tinsel and glitter disappear
Before the season has run.

It's too commercialised, it's lost its magic
I can't be bothered with this.
If it was crossed off the calendar from now on
It really wouldn't be missed.

We eat too much, we drink too much
We have to be happy and gay.
What I can say with all my heart is
Thank God for Boxing Day.

Christmas comes but once a year
Thank God it comes at all.
Without the hope and joy it brings
We would still be in the caul.

Thank God for the Angels and the glory,
The touching magic of the Christmas Story
The love, the care, the opening door,
The chance to live with him once more.

Thank God for the good will, health and cheer,
The chance to wish folk a Happy New Year.
Thank God for carols and hymns of praise,
The stars in the sky on which people can gaze.

Thank God for His star that lights our ways
To guide us to him at the end of our days
Here on Earth.

A E Norfolk

Christmas Shopping

Hustling, bustling, to the checkout till,
The harassed housewife faces the bill.
Has she got everything? Is anything missed?
The anaemic turkey was first on the list.
The trolleys piled high, will she need more?
Exhausting, frustrating, this tiresome chore;
Yet each year she does it, this last minute rush.
Can't Christmas be Christmas without all the fuss?

Jean Wallbank

A Christmas Box

Christmas had just one week to go
I was one of five puppies in a pet shop window,
People smiled at us as they passed by
We were all for sale for them to buy,
They rapped on the window and we all jumped about
'Aren't they beautiful,' we heard children shout.

The day came at last, I was lifted out
'Can I have that one, Dad?' I heard a little boy shout,
They took me home and made such a fuss
It was quite a long way 'cos we went on the bus.
They patted my head, said, 'What a nice pet.'
They didn't even grumble when I made the floor wet.

I was bathed and powdered and cuddled up close
Given pills and tablets and a medicine dose.
Christmas passed by, and then New Year's Day
Then I got the *gut* feeling I'm in the way.
No longer was I cuddled and then fussed over
I was just called *that dog* instead of *our Rover*.

I tried hard to be good, I was never sick
But now and again I received a sly kick,
There was one time when, I was locked out all night
It was freezing cold and I got such a fright.
They always fed me, one meal a day
But for some reason or other, no one wanted to play.

They were very quiet today, they turned me out in the wet
Put a string round my collar and took me down to the *vet*.
I *had* had all my jabs, against every infection
But they put me up on a table, gave me another injection,
I felt grand this morning, but now I feel lousy
My head's spinning round, I'm beginning to feel drowsy.

This is a very sad story, unfortunately it's true
You wouldn't like it if it happened to you.
So when *you* buy a pet, will you please remember
It's yours for life, not just for December.
When you read this, no doubt you will frown
I feel a bit tired, now I think I'll go and lie down.
I'm nearly asleep, but I really did try
I'll close my eyes now, God bless and Goodbye.

Jim Armstrong

Xmas Eve

The stockings hanging by the fire
Fill children's faces with desire,
What will Santa bring tonight?
And will he see without a light?

Mince pies and a glass of sherry
Mistletoe just to be merry
Will mum receive a kiss
from Santa that I will miss?

Sacks on the end of beds
Children laying down their heads,
Eyes trying not to close
Thinking of Rudolph and his red nose.

But all is quiet and still
As Santa comes, until
Morning light just begins to break
And happy children then awake.

Eve Calder

The Time of Year

Oh yes again it's Christmas time, a time for all to share.
To go out of our way, to show how much we care.
The joy of giving someone, this humble little gift.
Not only is it pleasure, but you really get a lift.
But if you ever listen to those with much to do
With very little meaning, that's why they feel so blue.
How often is it mentioned, of who will be asked to dine.
To show off all the splendid things, then upgrade it with the wine.
You rarely hear of people, who all the time will feed.
Those poor and humble little souls, who really have a need.
It's really most rewarding to spread yourself around
There is often someone lonely, who needs, that's what I have found.
If you ever notice the things that please us most of all,
Is very often simple, like a friendly soul to call.

M Truepenny

The Xmas Tree

Years roll on, it's December again,
And Xmas sings an old refrain.
Growing old, don't seem to care,
For the feeling once was there.
Why I bother, I just don't know,
But to the loft I have to go.
The tree is once again in place,
Something special it does embrace.
Lit up bells, with nursery rhyme,
Undiminished through passing time.
The fairy on top then has to be,
For the nine month girl there to see.
A Father Xmas in bright red
Got the little lad out of bed
Tinsel, lights, and a tiny toy
Was magic to our little boy.
Far away days, now long gone,
Endless Xmas's to dwell upon.
Somehow never seems to pall,
Thou' I thought I'd seen it all.
Why do it then? I ask,
This annual chore, Xmas task.
Wife, daughter, son and me,
Are all there in the Xmas tree.

D Baynes

Christmas

There's Christmas on the tele,
And Christmas in the shops.
There's Christmas food and Christmas drink,
And records in the Pops.

There's dozens of Christmas grottoes,
Father Christmas must be fun,
But paper hats and mottoes,
Are not for everyone.

There's families without money,
There's children without food.
No houses, and no shelter,
So why should life be good?

What's happened then to Christmas,
In this age of have it all?
Is the Christ child then forgotten,
Lying in the manger stall?

If you feel God's love around you,
If Christ's promise is your power.
Share that love with one another,
And the root of peace will flower.

For caring for each other,
At Christmas and all year,
Brings heaven on earth much closer,
And is truly Christmas cheer.

Doris Riding

Christmas Ghosts

As I sit alone in my room,
Surrounded by Christmas cheer,
There are ghosts in the corner's gloom
Who come and stand by my chair.

There's the ghost of love I knew
That died long ago,
Strangled by me before it grew
A frail, fragile thing I prized too much.

There's the ghost of a child I bore.
Where did he go?
Born with joy, here no more,
Killed in a war, too young to die.

Now comes the ghost of a hope
That lit all my days.
Put out and hung with the rope,
Hope was quenched long ago.

In each corner there is a ghost
Please, leave me alone
Go back, return to your post
It's Christmas and the time of good cheer.

Margery Horsburgh

Humour

Don't worry if the turkeys not cooked,
or the pudding still not made,
Christmas day will come and go
but memories will not fade,
Of you and I, and others too,
who made the loudest noise,
in past remembered parties of,
yuletide joys.

Mary Whittle

Oh! Lord is Christmas Here Again Already?

Oh! Lord is Christmas here again already?
When an outing to the shops becomes a war;
Sweet old ladies declare battle with sticks and brollies
Watch your shins they'll be coming back for more!

Mince pies are devoured en route to cake tins;
The end of sticky tape becomes obscure,
The tree lights flash (although they're not supposed to!)
Yet when guests arrive I will still appear demure.

When Santa's sure to put me in the poorhouse,
And the balloons have all shrivelled up like prunes,
When I've picked the tree up off the floor again,
Oh! how I crave for a tranquil afternoon.

Oh! Lord is Christmas here again already?
Give me the grace to hold my tongue and count to ten,
When I've tried to stuff the turkey twice in error,
And we've eaten and drank too much again.

So I'll take a moment to make my Christmas wish
That we may live in a world of peace and cheer,
And the joy upon the faces of the children of all races
Makes Christmas time a special time of year.

Caren Jayne

Why Fairies Top our Christmas Tree?

Father Christmas and a fairy
Are handing out trees to the needy
It's Christmas Eve and all seems well
But tomorrow morning will really tell.

As Christmas Eve comes to an end
The last of the needy who depend
On Santa's generosity, leaves
But look one's left I do believe.

The fairy turns to Santa Clause
I've one left over, there's a pause
What shall I do with it? she asks
Santa smiles and tells her the task

And that is why you'll always see
A fairy on top of your Christmas tree.

Colin Willis

Untitled

Prickly holly, mistletoe and wine
Arrange the food, it's Christmas Time
Our friends arrive, and singing Carols, divine
Turkey in the oven, is my neighbour's, not mine
We are invited in next door at five
The Turkey is not big enough, and not alive
What excuse we have, can only be applied
Saved by the bell, order some Chinese Fried.

Mary Bell

Christmas Crackers

Here's a seasonal yuletide cheer
Greetings and good tidings dear
Ho - Ho - Ho - Xmas is here.

Red nosed Reindeers led by Rudolph speed with sleighs far and near
Santa's visiting everyone - Everywhere.
Heavily laden with sackfulls of goodies - and gifts galore
In every single shopping centre - in Town and City store
Children chanting Christmas carols at the entrance of each door
And the good old band of hope - the sweet Sally Army singers
Following onwards - Valiantly - Despite the weather as ever before
Have a winter warming wine - or an ice-cood beer
Come and join us in our merriment - never fear.
It's the best brewed Brown Ale - refreshingly clear.
Commendably rich and fit for a peer.
It's a welcoming favourite straight from Newcastle's Brewery in
Tyne and Wear .

E Haydon Sanderson

The Dog's Dinner

My mother is daft you must agree
For on last Christmas Eve, you see
She put the turkey on to cook
Then fell asleep with her book.
Some hours later when she awoke
She found the house was full of smoke,
When she went to the oven to see
There were twenty-seven pounds of burnt turkey
With no shops open to buy another
It was Christmas chicken with my daft Mother.

Margaret Smythers

Christmas Day

The sound of young voices ends all sleeping,
Footsteps are heard and the stairs start creaking,
Soon everyone is up and moving about,
The kids are excited and scream and shout,
Lots of presents are under the tree,
They all call out 'Please open me!'
The kids open their presents as if in a race,
Expectation and joy fills each small face,
Then off they go to enjoy their new toys,
Causing havoc on the floor and plenty of noise,
And think of poor Mum on Christmas Day,
Stuck in the kitchen and slaving away,
She's stuffing the turkey and is up to her eyes,
With the making of dinner and lots of mince pies,
Dad helps later with serving and carves up the meat,
While everyone else scrambles madly to find a decent seat,
Relations come to visit you and chat for hours on end,
But will someone make you mad and drive you round the bend?
Soon it's getting really late and you want to get some sleep,
The day has been rather hectic and you collapse into a heap . . .

Stephen Norris

Wrong Day

Christmas Day, *Hoorah hoorah*.
The time for all good cheer.
It's not too hot - so another tot;
For a chaser! - one large beer.
Trees adorned with berried holly,
Some folk-a-singing - some in a flurry
The lights all ablaze - forget the worry.
I'm slightly tipsy sipping beer-n-whisky
While the church-bell rings the day.
Wife'y makes brave - she's *kitchen slave*.
I'm singing! - *The merry sleigh*.
No Santa yet in his fiery red
Everyone up - not a soul in bed.
Where is Santa? - has he lost his way,
Or is he boozed and sold his sleigh?
Nuts - crackers - you drunken hoaf
My wife began to say.
Today is only the twenty fourth,
He doesn't come, until one more day.

R L Bennett

Tarnished Tinsel

Christmas week I went out to the sales -
My *nose* for a bargain ne'er fails,
But, *Oh not again Mum - we don't want to come,*
My family protestingly wails.

Each shop was a challenge indeed,
Crowds pushed with insatiable greed.
It was just like a scrummage, the goods mostly rummage,
Tarnished tinsel festooned like a weed.

Despite the fact son said 'No way,'
He came out the best of the fray!
Red pyjamas and socks - stripy shirts in a box,
And that hated school sweater of grey!

Granny, usually so prim and so proper
Turned into a real demon shopper.
She poked and she prodded, whilst folks stood and nodded,
But no-one endeavoured to stop her!

For myself. How I needed a gin!
Footsore, weary and head in a spin.
To this caper now wise, satisfaction *my* prize -
Next year's presents just cheaply bought in!

Sue Caple

The Present

What a lovely thought, what a gift.
Was that right to say? - to stop a rift.
But what could I wear it with in daylight
to hide it, to stop giving horses a fright

Surely it looked like that in the shop.
It wouldn't even look right on a mop.
The colours weren't right - they clashed
Perhaps I'd wear it if I got smashed

The thing shouldn't have been made
The creator shouldn't have been paid
It may have been given as a joke
But no! They were sincere as they spoke.

How would I judge it when they called
To wear this thing that so appalled
Maybe I could to far lands emigrate
And throw away this thing I hate

Then with head beginning to sing
I saw they wore a similar thing
'That's nice' I said downing a beer
'Yes' they said 'from you last year'

John Wellings

A Teenage Hero Father Christmas

A little boy sat up in bed
To see a stranger cloaked in red
'Who are you?' asked the little boy,
And Santa turned round, aglow with joy,
'I'm Santa Claus, my little fellow . . .'
'Who's that?' asked the boy, 'Where's Donotello?'
'Mom said the Mutant Turtles would
Deliver my presents if I was good,
You're a fraud, I'd give you zero;
You're nothing like a Mutant Hero!'
The little boy pulled out his tongue
And sang the Teenage Turtle song,
He said, 'You're no Turtle, I can tell,
You haven't even got a shield.
You haven't got a shied or sword;
You're nothing but a silly fraud.
You can take all those toys back
If there's no Turtles in your sack!
Whether it's a trainset or talking doll called Myrtle,
It just isn't *HEP* unless it's a Turtle!'

Robert Hougton

Oozing with Christmas Spirit?!

Christmas, it comes but once a year;
Money, money, money; has gone; is no more,
The children, they enjoy, and a glorious cheer.
Decorating ones tree, gold lavish laden high;
Expense, expense, I really could cry!

Wandering around; a Scrooge like manner,
Snowballs are hurling towards my head,
Wishing; dreaming of holding a hard banner;
The snowball throwers; yes, they would have fled.

An established fact; it's only once a year
My lord thank goodness, *oh dear*,
Misery, that we surely are;
For us old Scrooges it brings nothing but fear!

Christmas joy and Christmas spirit;
We've seen the *spirit* and that's for sure!
An extravaganza of food and drink,
The carrot and wine, Santa is withering on the brink.

Ignoring Christmas festivity fun,
New Year coming our way,
Acting like a Scrooge at Christmas,
But Christmas is a good price to pay!

Tony Watson

Christmas Humour

Santa Santa we love you.
The snow is not deep
I know you'll get thro'
Your Reindeer if like horses
Will racedown Sandown Park to No 12.
Karl Hayley Graham and Oliver
Are waiting for you
The Xmas tree is full of lights
And a fairy too.
Please climb down our chimney
As it's been cleaned for you
Our mum Helen has made mince pies
Roast turkey and plum pudding too.
Fruit drinks fruit cake just for you
Merry Xmas to Rudolph and you.
Remember Jesus in a stable
I bet he would visit us if he was able
To give us our pressies
And eat at our table
Santa Santa we love you.

Erimar MacMillan

Xmas Shopping

Hustle, bustle,
Wrappings rustle,
Tinsels glitter,
Children twitter,
People coming,
People going,
Pushing, running, calling, shouting
Cheery greetings in their meetings.
Mother's natter - what's the matter?
Xmas shopping!
That's what is!
And as always I am saying
I'll shop early next time round.
I won't be a part of this
The humping, bumping, and the wails
Next time I'll shop early -
In the January Sales!

Caroline Shore

Christmas Shopping

Shopping, shopping what a spree,
Hubby and I set off with glee,
In and out the shops so bright
All aglow with Christmas light,
Candles here and baubles there,
Look at that great teddy bear.
Tinsel on the Christmas tree
Santa with a child upon his knee.
Just look at that Nativity Scene
A beautiful sight that's ever been.
There's magic in the air alright.
'Til hubby says 'I want a bite'
All this hurrying and scurrying around
Your feet have hardly touched the ground,
I think you'd better rest my dear!
Good job *he* only comes but *once* a year.

Mona Bulmer

A Very Happy Christmas

'Have a very happy Christmas' is that what you say?
It's obvious you haven't got a family like mine for the day.
There's Uncle George, Aunty Mabel, Gran and Granpa to name a
few

Then there's my favourite niece Ellie who will bring her two
Her husband comes later after the lunchtime drinking
A *Very Happy Christmas* is not what I'm thinking.
My Mother and Father will bring sister Kate
Although the dinner is all ready they are bound to be late
Oh why, oh why, did I have to say
Come over for Christmas, we will have a nice day
Aunt Mabel and Mother will sit and watch telly
While Uncle George and Dad will be feeding their bellies
Ellie's husband spreads himself out and continues to drink
Whilst I will be permanently stuck to the sink
The children will be fighting instead of quietly playing
'Have a very Happy Christmas' is that what your saying?
I'll really go away for Christmas next year
Or I'll have them for every Christmas I fear
Why do I have them? Why come to me?
I suppose the fact is I love them all you see
Now they are leaving full of good cheer
Saying *Thanks for a nice time same place next year?*

J Roberts

The Real Story

Christmas comes but all too soon
decorations on sale since early June,
hustle and bustle all round the shops
pushing and shoving and losing young tots.

Fighting in stores to get last minute toys
dolls for the girls and cars for the boys,
socks and hankies for dad every year
what he really wants is a barrel of beer.

Then comes the big day we've all waited for
kids playing with boxes and gifts on the floor,
mums fluffy slippers are far too tight
and gran in her curlers is looking a sight.

Everyone's screaming re what's on the telly
getting drunk in the corner is old auntie Nellie,
then all goes quiet for watching the Queen
repeats are on later, we've already seen.

And when the day's over mum puts up her feet
Opening chocolates she can't really eat,
Having eaten and drunk until in great pain
Recovering in time to do it all over again.

Alison Downie

Christmas Day Visit

Bell rings, cold fingers clutching magic
in gaily wrapped parcels at the door,
family get together, hugging, laughing
mindful of what the season's for.

Ethel eagerly relates her recent illness
must break away, make that pot of tea,
burnt mince pies cringe under icing sugar
seems like a good disguise to me.

I'm certainly stunned with uncle's present
long negligee, cerise and sheer,
really can't think what came over him
he only brought wine gums last year.

They are arguing football in the corner
our yorkshire terrier's just been sick,
young Nigel's head is in the fridge
while my cousin shows his latest trick.

Dad leads us off in carol singing
uneasy peace surrounds the room,
I place fixed smile upon my face -
hubby's bought me the wrong perfume.

G Price

The Christmas Tree

One day a Christmas tree went for a walk.
And he met his old friend the yew.
Poo, said the latter with great disgust.
You look absurd, *'tis true*,
Fancy them decorating you like that.
With tinsel and silver balls
And a fairy doll up on your head,
You know she'll break if she falls.
My friend, the yew 'tis worth it
To watch the children's pleasure
As they undo each little parcel -
And find in it a treasure.

Rita Vincent

News Flash

Attention, all children!
A mystery virus has struck
the toymakers in Greenland.
Father Christmas, is having
to do the work alone.
He regrets, he may be late
arriving, at your home.

Attention, all children!
Please don't get up early, on
Christmas morning, this year.
Parents have told us, Father
Christmas, says he'll be late
so there is really no point
in you waking up, before eight.

But if you do (and you will)
Please try to be quiet.
At two o'clock, some parents
(strangely) are still tired!

Sue Bevin

Untitled

Mum - this year I promise I won't repeat
The whoopee cushion I put on your seat
Or fuse the Christmas tree lights.
I'll stuff the turkey and not the cat
Won't call Aunt Ethel a boring old prat
Or eat all the turkish delights.

Anne Lamb

Untitled

'Christmas is humbug' said Mr Scrooge
In a way I suppose he was right.
The shops are so busy, the bills are so huge
Through the crowds you have to fight.
What to buy, is racking our brain.
Just writing the cards, is another pain.
And wrapping the parcel up all posh.
O'h if only we had lots of dosh.
Mr Scrooge, you were a strange bloke,
If we were rich instead of broke
We'd organise some parties and give a treat
Invite all the people off the street,
As this cannot be, my friends I shall see
And wish them all the best.
Merry Christmas everyone.

Christine Rodgers

Warmest Wishes

The freezing fog holds Christmas
in its ruthless, icy grip;
all day the roofs stay frosty,
while on pavements people slip.
Absent all of Christmas Day
is one important guest:
detained in warmer climes, the sun
sends all his very best!

Michael L G Bailey

Things That Go Jump in the Night

Christmas is a busy time with lots of things to do.
Trees to dress and gifts to wrap, *with love from me to you.*

What can we buy Caroline? I cannot think at all.
Don't really know what size she is, or even just how tall.

Just when I was giving up and wondering what to do
A little bird came on the scene and offered a helpful clue.

It came a little closer and said 'Caroline's into frogs'
Frogs? yes, little green things that usually sit on logs.

So off I *frog-marched* to the shops to see what I could find.
I saw brown bears and little pink pigs, but not a frog of *any* kind.

Then I spied a pencil box covered in you know what.
I asked had she any other frogs. She said 'no that's your lot'.

Then I found a froggy soap and a froggy bubble bath.
By now I was having cobs of fun and also a jolly good laugh.

Town was very crowded - people rushed and pushed a bit.
I could have *leapfrogged* over them but haven't got the knees for it.

By chance I passed another shop and there, high upon a shelf
Sat a lovely little frog - alone - all by himself.

I asked the lady for the frog and paid the price on the tag.
Freddy the frog took one long jump, two back flips and landed in my
                                                                            bag.

So at the moment he's in the bath sitting upon a lily.
Isn't this poem ridiculous? In fact, it's just plain silly.
Croak! Croak! Croak!

E Spinks

A Thought for Xmas

It's Christmas time so spare a thought,
Take a look at all the things you've brought,
Then think of those who won't get any,
Not even a sweet for a penny.
But please don't say 'I don't care',
Just spare,
A thought for them at Christmas time.

Clare Barnett

Three Wishes

Soft, gentle, I saw the snow fall
Load and clear, I heard the Robin call
The boughs of holly hanging in the hall
Snugly lies a baby in his manger stall
Three wishes of peace, joy and love to all
These simple words so easy to recall
Are forgotten because man needs to destroy all.

Norma Tate

Christmas Lunch at the Day Hospital

We've been celebrating Christmas
Enthusiastically
It's had a strange effect on us
As you can plainly see!

We came here to The Day Centre
To have our Christmas lunch.
The pudding filled us with a glow
It's full of Christmas punch!

The plates were filled with turkey
And other Christmas fayre
Instead of tea... a sherry mmm,
We haven't got a care!
We're full of Christmas spirit
We know it won't be long,
We're feeling so elated,
'Fore breaking into song!

We can see a lot of stars and lights
In front of all our eyes
Perhaps they're real, perhaps they're caused
By eating rich mince pies!
The welcome shown by Sister
And all her merry crew
Has really set the atmosphere
And warmed us through and through
They're Christmas crackers everyone
And filled with Christmas cheer!
The proof we've all enjoyed ourselves?
We're coming back *next year!*

Gwen Barton

An Orphan's Wish

I look into the window
And I know I can't be seen,
The family, they're so engrossed
They'll never know I've been.

They're opening Xmas presents
On this cold and frosty morn'
Laughing, happy and surprised
Are expressions that are worn.

Logs are in the fireplace
The table is all set
Turkey is in the oven
For the meal they've soon to get.

I can't help feeling jealous
I wipe away a tear
I'd love to have a family
For this one day of the year.

The children's home's not that bad
I feel I have to say
But oh to have a family
For especially Xmas Day.

Janis Robertson

To Kevin at Christmas

I don't know if they've told you
I think perhaps they should
That Father Christmas never comes
It's no use being good.

They can't help it, my darling
They've done the best they can
Your mummy's got no money
And neither has her man.

Your daddy's out in limbo
He's rotting on the shelf
He doesn't bother writing
He's thinking of himself.

I think they should have told you
It's hard enough to live
Forget the sledge and reindeer
And sacks of toys to give.

Still, never mind my lovely
You have a happy day
There'll be a lot of drink about
And someone has to pay.

Raine Marriner

Suffer Little Children

On those wintry nights
With Christmas nigh
And your own young folk
Home and dry
Think of those children
Locked in hell
Petrified with bomb and shell
Starved of food
And love as well
No Santa Claus
To greet the day
With presents great
And laughter gay
Only the grim reapers box
Instead of Santa's
Christmas socks.

Roy Whitfield

Once Again

It's the time of year again
When keeping secrets can be a pain
Hiding presents out of eyes view
Sending cards to relations and friends so true
Seeking out the decorations that you neatly put away
Only to find some have decaded
The tree you brought has dropped all over the floor
Next year, you say, never, no more
We'll buy a silk one, they look just as real
And they last forever and to the eyes they do appeal
You spend ages buying presents, the kids will like
But they prefer the boxes not the new bikes
And when dinner is over and you're full to the brim
You try to sleep it off, but the kid won't let you win
Struggling though until stars come out at night
So the children sleep tucked up, warm and tight
Next year they will be older so it should be better
I must remember to send Santa a thank you letter.

J Nice

Dear Father Christmas

Dear Father Christmas, what's it all about?
Everybody rushing round looking full of doubt,
What shall we buy for Uncle Mick?
Would Grandpa like a new walking stick.
Shall we have turkey or shall we have goose?
Don't the fairy lights work, they must be loose.
What shall we have at the top of the tree?
A fairy or a star to see.
When at last the day draws nigh,
We'll tick our check list and heave a sigh.
Trimmings are up, what a sight to see!
Presents are wrapped and under the tree,
Turkey's in the oven, don't let it burn,
Puddings are mixed, we've all had a turn.
Open our presents from such a such,
Enjoy ourselves and eat too much,
Snooze in the chair after lunch,
We really are a peculiar bunch.
Nevertheless it was really great,
Next year seems such a long while to wait.

Jan Lowe

What can I Get?

'Mum, what can I get Dad for Christmas?
'Don't ask me, I've run out of ideas
He doesn't smoke, he doesn't drink and has a draw full of socks'.
'What about a tie? - or hankies?
'Hardly uses them!'
'Slippers?'
'Hasn't started on last year's yet!
The car's shabby, he could do with a new one of those!
'Or a trip on the moon, I suppose'
'No, he's not keen on flying'
'You're not helping much are you?'
'I told you I'd run out of ideas'
'Shall I get a book then?'
'Its as much as he can do to scan the daily papers!'
'A voucher?'
'Too boring!'
'Oh well, it will have to be socks again!'
'That's right dear, he'll enjoy that!'

Margaret Aitken

Christmas Humour

It's Christmas Day around the tree,
We gather together the family.
There's Mum whose face is alight with pleasure
For now she's retired and can sit back at leisure.
There's my other half looking full of good cheer,
He needs no excuse now that Christmas is here.
There's my only son having such lovely fun,
My daughter who now has her own little ones.
My son-in-law there, looking on in despair,
At his sons doing battle with each others hair.
With my loved ones gathered around that tree,
What could I wish for more?
Only that we would be lucky enough to have many more.

Muriel Palmer

The Fairy

While walking through the garden, one lovely sunny day.
I thought I saw a fairy, in a flower she lay.
I stood there in amazement, I didn't know what to say.
So I held my breath in case a sign should frighten her away.
A tiny gorgeous little thing. I couldn't believe my eyes.
Her hair was gold like strands of silk, her wings were golden too.
Her dress was like a pretty flower, a lovely shade of blue.
And as I gazed in wonder, a bee came buzzing by,
He seemed to whisper in her ear and then away it flew.
Then she awoke and saw me there and upwards she did fly.
Flew round my head three times die she then blew gently in my eye.
Then I awoke to find myself lying on the ground.
Had I dreamt all this and thought and slowly looked around.
And then I thought I saw the flower in which she had been lain.
So what was this a spiders web or was it a golden skein.
I took it home and pressed it in the pages of a book.
And I have it to this very day if you would care to look.
Oh! I believe in fairies, yes indeed I do.
If you were me all those years ago, wouldn't you.

June Linacre

Untitled

Little man, little man, though your only a babe.
You were sent by god above for the whole world to save.

With those beasts so low - a stable you did share.

If only they could speak.
What tales they would tell.
Of a nation, oh so meek.

Of strife and of war it was foretold.
Why men try so hard - to be so bold.

If man were pushed - of bomb C.N.D.
With a finger so cold.

A war to end, war of all wars.
Were to begin.
Would you intervene.

You were given from above.
With Mary's good grace.
God sent you with his love.

Julie March

Delilah II

(or a Christmas visit to the Barbers in South Shields the following year)

Different barbers the following year.
These unisex ladies wore different gear.
All dressed up as Father Christmas.
Complete with shorts, thighs what a prize.

Snip, Snip, Snip, Snip, Snip, Snip.
This Christmas has
This Christmas has
Provided my own dear Stockton lass.

K Chesney-Woods

Christmas Day 1962

Nineteen Sixty Two was a good year celebrating Christmas cheer
I was very merry, my belly full of beer
So drunk was I (after Christmas dinner) I went to bed
I couldn't really remember eating my turkey leg
I remember dreaming of Santa Claus
In Nineteen Sixty Two, nobody dreamt of evil wars
I remember dreaming of all the best
Sonny Liston, The Beatles and Beau Geste
I remember lots about Christmas of Sixty Two
Getting up from bed to go to the loo
Going back to bed and dreamin' on
You'd think I was Sid James in a Christmas carry on
Tossing and turning I felt my head rubbing
I awoke to the smell of Christmas pudding
My wife brought me a plateful on a tray
She said 'so this is how a drunkard spends Christmas Day'
I apologised for behaving like a skunk
She bellowed 'You're no skunk - just drunk'
I laughed and said 'darling don't be hard'
Just 'giss' a kiss my Christmas card.

P Durow

Star Glazing at Christmas

Merry Christmas to you all
Not just you
But the Christmas cake,
Mince pies
And the mulled wine to,
Merry Christmas to you all
The Celestial Planets are bright
In the skies above
At this time of year.
They must be having a Merry
Christmas to
Mulled wine.

David Bratley

Untitled

Xmas will soon be here
With all its fun and gravilities
And with the lights upon the tree
For all of us to see.

The star that shines on the toy
And the tinsel too
And with the little balls that
Hang on every branch you see.

Oh what a jog it is to see
All this and many more
The people sitting by the fireside
All sharing presents on Xmas morn'.

P Gordon

Father Christmas

I saw Father Christmas,
Sitting red-faced on a chair.
His hair the colour of soot.
This special man did sit and stare,
Not like him to loiter there.
Then he got up and paced about,
Looking like a silly lout,
I realised, he had burnt his bum.
Then into the room,
Who should appear, but mum.

Father Christmas pulled his trousers down,
Mum rubbed cream on the sore spot.
Nobody made a sound,
Except me.
I laughed and laughed,
Until I was tired.
Then I went to bed,
But could not sleep,
Because that amusing picture,
Kept going round and round in my head.

L K Webster

Christmas Tribute to Dad

Dad you were a very patient man,
Saintly through and through.
Always there to show your care,
For others in everything you would say and do.

Through you God's love would shine so true,
If I needed to talk or support, I could rely on you,
You were a rock the whole year through,
But Christmas was special at Grandma and Granddad's with you.

We cheerily went along to church to sing Christmas praises.
At Grandma's house, one of my favourite places,
Father Christmas came, you should have seen our smiles,
As we opened our toys and pulled crackers under the Christmas
    tree,
With my two sisters. They were times of happiness and hilarity.
You were a thoughtful Dad beating others by many miles,
I loved to sit and cuddle you sat upon your knee.

You were so full of life even though later you became so ill,
Though you were called away to Heaven I can feel your spirit still,
Guiding me and helping me to say and do what is best and right.
Celebrating Jesus' birthday makes me feel hopeful, happy and high,
Especially knowing we will meet again at his feet, in paradise above
    the sky.

Kevin E Sims

Advent Hopes

Optimistically each Christmas
Despite all past experiences,
I shake my apron of procrastination
Free from creases and deep folds of idleness,
Aim at the mythic fiction of perfection,
To tame the fiery chimera of domesticity,
which skeeters, claws rattling,
Across the clean mopped tiles.
By Christmas Eve reality,
Intrudes in its totality,
The perfect housewife, dragon winged,
Slides out my grasp and slithers off,
In search of more hospitable
Homes than mine - I'm left
With only fuming alcoholic breaths
Blazing haphazardly around
The Christmas pudding and igniting
The holly and the paper decorations,
Yet another triumph of
Experience over hope.

J Wright

Mother Alone

It wasn't an easy path my mother chose to take
It wasn't an easy choice for anyone to make
She fed and clothed and nurtured us
Year in, year out and never fussed.

It was an uphill struggle, pitfalls on the way
Only someone strong as her would battle on each day
Financially things were bad, but emotionally we were strong.
Funny when you look around, some have the money,
But the other bit is gone!

Mother alone you did a great job,
You might as well be two,
Mum and Dad rolled into one,
Just thanks for being you.

Barbara Eassom

Untitled

There's Mothers the whole world over
With hearts that beat so true
But there will never be another Mum
More wonderful than you.

E Dall

A Young Boy's Secret

At dawn on Christmas Eve when all was quiet,
I sneaked down the stairs and into the pantry.
We had no fridge then and I cut cubes,
the size of a dice, off my Dad's favourite cheese,
It smelt strong and was deep blue in mould.
Holding my breath I crept back upstairs,
and after opening the window so carefully,
I catapulted the cubes into the cool,
looking dark water of the canal.
Then after a few minutes, on this still festive day,
the water began to ripple and broke into a swirl
and this great fish appeared,
bump backed and splendid in firey colours,
He rolled on the surface blowing and slurping
'til the cheese was all gone.
Then I ate the last piece and went back to sleep,
and dreamt of my new rod,
and how I might catch this cold blooded wonder,
at the back of our house.

David Quick

Christmas Eve

Christmas Eve is here at last,
Excitement knows no bounds,
Baubles shining on the tree,
And tinsel all around.
Children's happy faces,
Getting ready for bed,
For to dream of Santa Claus,
When their prayers are said,
Leave mince pies for Santa,
And a glass of wine,
Shout the merry children,
For he needs to dine.
Tucked in bed by Mum and Dad,
To children soundly sleep,
And wait for Santa Claus to come,
To fill their stockings deep.

Ruby Anderson

Seasons

Christmas is over and New Year has begun,
Now we can look forward to spring, then summer sun,
Autumn then will come around, then winter once again,
Oh how I wish that spring and summer,
All year would with us remain.

The warmer weather cheers you up,
And makes you feel good too,
You get out and visit places, that before you never knew,
Faces smiling to match the sun instead of cold and sad,
These are the things I love to see, these things make me glad.

I know the festive season, makes up for the winter cold,
But snow and ice are for the young,
Not pleasure when you're old.

So have a lovely year all round, what each season brings,
Make the most of what it brings, when the birdies sing,
Soon the winter will be back,
And all those festive things, then the circle starts again,
After the New Years bells ring.

Grace Clark